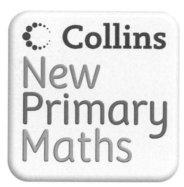

Collins New Primary Maths

Pupil Book 4A

Series Editor: Peter Clarke

Authors: Jeanette Mumford, Sandra Roberts, Andrew Edmondson

Contents

Fun four-digits

● Partition, round and order four-digit numbers

1 Make the number from its parts. 2000 + 500 + 40 + 6 makes 2546

a 6000 + 900 + 20 + 4 makes

b 3000 + 200 + 90 + 7 makes

c 4000 + 200 makes

2 Write the number that each red digit represents. 5874   800

a 4923   b 3260

c 1684   d 6759

e 1059   f 5411

1 Add these parts to make a number.

a 70   8   b 20   5000   c 4000   1

200   4000   3   600   80

2 Round the red numbers to the nearest 10.

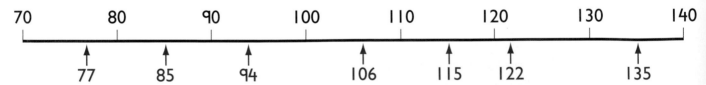

3 Round the green numbers to the nearest 10.

Round these numbers to the nearest 10.

a 1325   b 2467   c 1073
d 2122   e 2591   f 1996

Jewel numbers

● **Add or subtract mentally pairs of two-digit numbers**

1 Add these pairs of numbers.

a | 27 | 35

b | 39 | 41

c | 56 | 24

d | 87 | 35

e | 67 | 44

f | 58 | 19

g | 23 | 91

h | 12 | 77

2 Now subtract the smaller number from the larger one.

Write four addition and four subtraction calculations using two-digit numbers to give the answers on the jewels.

 65

 78

 59

 86

 93

 76

 78

Example

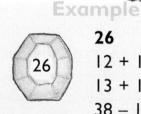

26

26

$12 + 14 = 26$

$13 + 13 = 26$

$38 - 12 = 26$

$39 - 13 = 26$

What two-digit calculations can you make using the digits 1, 6, 8 and 3? For example: $16 + 38 = 54$. What do you notice about your answers? Why is this?

Use your facts!

● **Use knowledge of addition and subtraction facts**

 Choose two calculations that go together, one from each bucket. Then write the answers to both calculations.

6 + 2
4 + 3
8 − 3
5 + 4
9 + 3
13 − 5
7 + 6
12 − 4
9 + 5
14 − 6
4 + 9

Example

6 + 2 = 8
60 + 20 = 80

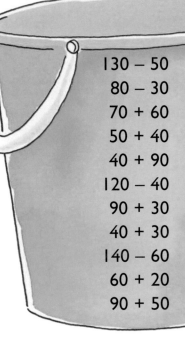

130 − 50
80 − 30
70 + 60
50 + 40
40 + 90
120 − 40
90 + 30
40 + 30
140 − 60
60 + 20
90 + 50

 Choose three calculations that go together, one from each bucket. Then write the answers to all three calculations.

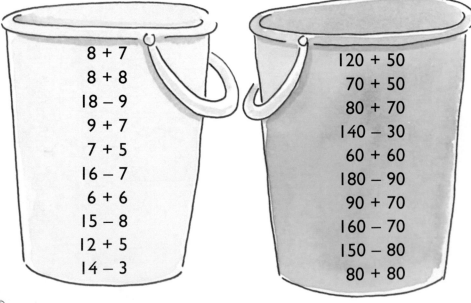

8 + 7
8 + 8
18 − 9
9 + 7
7 + 5
16 − 7
6 + 6
15 − 8
12 + 5
14 − 3

120 + 50
70 + 50
80 + 70
140 − 30
60 + 60
180 − 90
90 + 70
160 − 70
150 − 80
80 + 80

1200 + 500
800 + 800
900 + 700
1400 − 300
1500 − 800
800 + 700
700 + 500
1600 − 700
1800 − 900
600 + 600

 Explain why these calculations go together.

Key it in

- **Use a calculator to carry out one-step and two-step calculations**

Use the calculator to work out these calculations. Enter the numbers carefully!

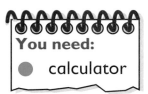

You need:
- calculator

a 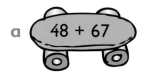 48 + 67

d 75 − 8

g 16 × 3

b 79 + 81

e 93 − 81

h 36 × 4

c 78 + 39

f 142 − 91

i 56 ÷ 7

j 96 ÷ 8

Use the calculator to work out these calculations. Enter the numbers carefully!

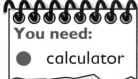

You need:
- calculator

a 482 + 684 =

b 752 + 914 =

c 847 + 654 =

d 7458 − 657 =

e 863 − 752 =

f 831 − 458 =

g 49 × 7 =

h 98 × 6 =

i 57 × 14 =

j 261 × 75 =

k 104 ÷ 13 =

l 369 ÷ 9 =

Remember

Check your answers!

What would these calculator displays be when written as money?

You need:
- calculator

a 4.62

b 3.21

c 1.09

d 5.77

e 8.12

f 10.51

Constantly counting

● **Recognise positive and negative numbers and position them on a number line**

Copy and complete the number lines.

a −4 ☐ −2 ☐ 0 1 ☐ ☐ ☐ ☐

b ☐ −5 ☐ −3 ☐ −1 0 ☐ 2 3 ☐

c ☐ −7 ☐ −5 ☐ ☐ −2 −1 0 1 ☐

d ☐ ☐ ☐ 0 ☐ 2 ☐ ☐ 5

1 Write these numbers out in order from highest to lowest.

a −4, −3, −8, −1, 0, −9
b 6, −7, 1, −2, 3, −6
c 0, 10, −1, 4, 7, −7
d 7, −4, 6, −8, 5, 1
e −3, 2, 0, −11, −8, 5
f −2, −8, −6, 5, 8, 12

2 Copy and complete the number line.

☐ −5 ☐ −3 ☐ −1 0 1 ☐ 3 ☐

Use your calculator to count backwards in 2s, starting from:

a − 0
b − 3
c − 8

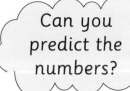

Can you predict the numbers?

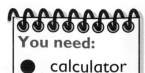

You need:
● calculator

Travel numbers

● **Recognise and continue patterns**

1 Copy and complete the number sequences.

a 11, 13, 15, 17, ___, ___, 23, 25, ___, ___

b 12, 16, 20, ___, 28, 32, ___, ___, ___, ___

c 1, 5, 9, 13, ___, ___, ___, ___, ___, ___

d 59, 61, 63, ___, ___, ___, ___, ___, 75, ___

e 44, 40, ___, ___, ___, 24, ___, 16, ___, ___

f ___, ___, 28, 31, 34, 37 ___, ___, ___

2 Add 2 to each of these numbers. Continue until you have written 8 numbers in each sequence.

a 82　　b 56　　c 97

d 31　　e 100　　f 75

3 Add 4 to each of these numbers. Continue until you have written 8 numbers in each sequence.

a 30　　b 27　　c 56

d 85　　e 96　　f 34

These buses started their journey with the number of people shown on each bus. They picked up 4 people at every bus stop. Write how many people are on each bus after each stop. The bus is full after 10 stops.

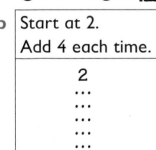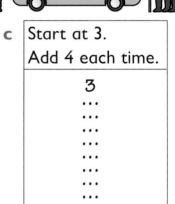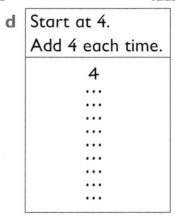

a Start at 1. Add 4 each time.	b Start at 2. Add 4 each time.	c Start at 3. Add 4 each time.	d Start at 4. Add 4 each time.
1 5 … … … … … … … …	2 … … … … … … … … …	3 … … … … … … … … …	4 … … … … … … … … …

Look carefully at the **units** digits in each list above. Write them out.

a What patterns can you see?

b Which patterns are the same?

c Which patterns are different?

Example

a 1, 5, …, …, …, …

b 2, …, …, …, …, …

c 3, …, …, …, …, …

d 4, …, …, …, …, …

Multiplication scores

● Know by heart multiplication facts for the 2, 3, 4, 5 and 10 times tables

Write two matching multiplication facts and addition facts.

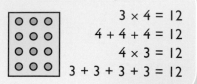

Example

$3 \times 4 = 12$
$4 + 4 + 4 = 12$
$4 \times 3 = 12$
$3 + 3 + 3 + 3 = 12$

a   **b**   **c**

e   **f**   **g**

d

Follow the rules to calculate the score for each dart thrown.

Example

$3 \times 2 = \square$ $8 \times 3 = \square$
$5 \times 10 = \square$ $7 \times 10 = \square$

a 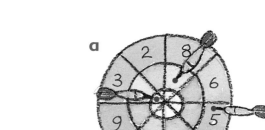   **b** 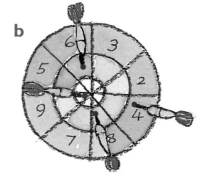   **c**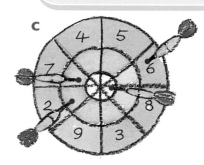

Darts Rules		**Darts Rules**		**Darts Rules**	
White:	× 2	White:	× 5	White:	× 3
Yellow:	× 3	Yellow:	× 4	Yellow:	× 4
Green:	× 10	Green:	× 2	Green:	× 5

Copy and complete the multiplication calculations.

a $4 \times 5 = \square$ **b** $6 \times 3 = \square$ **c** $7 \times 2 = \square$ **d** $8 \times 10 = \square$ **e** $5 \times 5 = \square$

f $8 \times 4 = \square$ **g** $9 \times 3 = \square$ **h** $8 \times 2 = \square$ **i** $7 \times 5 = \square$ **j** $10 \times 10 = \square$

k $\square \times 3 = 21$ **l** $\square \times 4 = 24$ **m** $4 \times \square = 32$ **n** $5 \times \square = 40$ **o** $\square \times 8 = 16$

Sweet facts

● **Derive quickly division facts relating to the 2, 3, 4, 5 and 10 times tables**

Write two multiplication and two division facts for each picture.

Example

3 × 5 = 15
5 × 3 = 15
15 ÷ 5 = 3
15 ÷ 3 = 5

a

b

c

d

e

Write a division fact to show how many squares of chocolate are in each row.
Write the multiplication fact you can use to check your answer.

Example

15 ÷ 3 = 5   3 × 5 = 15

a

b

c

d

e

f

g

h

Copy and complete the division calculations.

a 32 ÷ 4 = ☐   **b** 18 ÷ 3 = ☐   **c** 25 ÷ 5 = ☐   **d** 70 ÷ 10 = ☐   **e** 14 ÷ 2 = ☐

f 27 ÷ 3 = ☐   **g** 16 ÷ 4 = ☐   **h** 90 ÷ 10 = ☐   **i** 20 ÷ 2 = ☐   **j** 40 ÷ 5 = ☐

k 45 ÷ ☐ = 9   **l** 12 ÷ ☐ = 6   **m** ☐ ÷ 3 = 7   **n** ☐ ÷ 10 = 4   **o** 30 ÷ ☐ = 6

11

Multiplying and dividing by 10 and 100

● **Multiply and divide whole numbers by 10 and 100**

Multiply the number shown on each calculator by 10 and 100.

a  **15**   b  **8**   c  **12**   d  **30**   e  **14**

f  **9**   g  **20**   h  **16**   i  **10**   j  **19**

Copy and complete the tables.

a

Number	x 10	x 100
8	80	800
14		
685		
26		
3		
452		
987		
68		

b

Number	÷ 10	÷ 100
400		
800		
1200		
3500		
5800		
65 000		
51 000		
93 000		

Each of the following calculations have either been multiplied or divided by 10 or 100. Copy and complete.

a 630 $\boxed{}$ = 63   e 9200 $\boxed{}$ = 92

b 720 $\boxed{}$ = 7200   f 188 $\boxed{}$ = 18 800

c 42 $\boxed{}$ = 4200   g 1520 $\boxed{}$ = 15 200   i 3100 $\boxed{}$ = 310 000

d 66 000 $\boxed{}$ = 660   h 700 $\boxed{}$ = 7   j 1230 $\boxed{}$ = 123

Doubles and halves

Double two-digit numbers and work out the related halves

1 Double each of the numbers below.
Write an addition and multiplication fact for each.

Example

20 + 20 = 40
2 × 20 = 40

2 Halve each of the even numbers above. Write a division fact for each.

Example

20 ÷ 2 = 10

1 Double each of the numbers below.

2 Halve each of the numbers below.

1 Double each of the numbers below.

52 39 87 76 63 94 48 75

2 Halve each of the numbers below.

86 78 52 94 48 36 74 92

Cake addition

● Use addition facts to add multiples of 10 or 100

① Look at the cakes.
Write 10 addition
calculations using
two of the numbers.

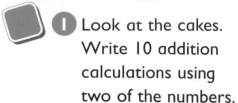

② Write 10 addition calculations using
three of the numbers.

Example

① Look at the cakes. Make up 10 calculations
adding two of the numbers together.

② Write 10 addition calculations using three of the numbers.

Write two tips to help when adding multiples of 10 or 100.

Biscuit subtraction

● **Use subtraction facts to subtract multiples of 10 or 100**

1 Look at the biscuits. Write 10 subtraction calculations using two of the numbers.

2 How many ways can you complete this calculation using numbers from the biscuits? □ − 30 = □.

Example

80 − 20 = 60

1 Look at the biscuits. Write 15 subtraction calculations using two of the numbers.

2 How many ways can you complete this calculation using numbers from the biscuits?
□ − 300 = □.

Explain a good method for checking calculations.

Consecutive numbers

● Investigate and test a statement

Statement:

Every number can be made by adding two consecutive numbers.

1 Can you make these numbers by adding two consecutive numbers?

Show your working.

12   27   38   49

52   79   81   97

2 Now choose some of your own numbers to try. What have you noticed?

1 Can you make these numbers by adding two consecutive numbers?

99   87   127   136

185   263   250   341

2 Is the statement true or false? Explain your reasons to prove what you think.

What two consecutive numbers added together total 1073?
Show how you would work it out.

Number order

Identify and use patterns, relationships and properties of numbers

- Using each digit card once only, make some 3-digit numbers.
- Write the numbers you have made in order, starting with the smallest.
- Repeat four more times.

Example

8	5	1
4	3	9
7	6	0

In order: 439, 760, 851

Use the digit cards 0-9 to make 3-digit numbers.

1
- Using each card once only, make the three largest numbers possible and write them down.
- Now make the three smallest numbers possible and write them down.

2
- Make five even numbers and write them down. Now write them again in order, starting with the smallest.
- This time make five odd numbers and write them down. Write the numbers in order, starting with the smallest.

3 Using each card once only:
- Make a multiple of 5.
- Make a multiple of 10.
- Make a multiple of 4.
- Make a multiple of 3.

4
- What is the largest 5-digit number you can make?
- What is the smallest 5-digit number you can make?

 Explain how you make the largest possible number with a set of 0-9 digit cards.

Fairground problems

● **Solve one-step and two-step word problems**

Merry-go-round £1.35

Dodgems £2.20

Big Wheel £2.85

Use the prices to work out the answers to the problems.

a Sally has £2 to spend. What ride can she go on and how much change will she get?

b Ben rides on the merry-go-round and the dodgems. How much does he spend?

c Mary buys a small drink and a toffee apple. How much does she spend?

d Jake has £5 to spend. He buys a hamburger. How much does he have left?

e Theo wants to have one turn on each of the rides. How much money will he need?

Hamburger £1.80

Small Cola 90p

Large Cola £1.15

a Grace has a ride on the big wheel and then gets a hamburger. How much does she spend?

b Nick wants two rides on the dodgems and pays with a £10 note. What will his change be?

c Max and Amy each have a ride on the dodgems and then on the big wheel. How much have they both spent altogether?

d Steve buys a small drink for himself and a large drink for his dad. He pays with a £20 note. How much change will he get?

e Tim has two rides at the fair. He spends £3.55. What were the two rides?

Toffee apple 75p

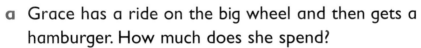

Write a two-step word problem for a friend to answer using the information on this page. You must work out the answer as well!

Easy sixes

● **Work out the 6 times table facts by doubling the 3 times table**

Find all the multiples of 3 in the treasure chest.
Then write the times table fact for each multiple.

Complete each times table fact for 3.
Look inside each card to find a times table fact for 6.
Double your first answer to complete the times table fact for 6.

a 2×3 2×6

b 5×3 5×6

c 3×3 3×6

d 8×3 8×6

e 6×3 6×6

f 9×3 9×6

Copy and complete the division calculations.

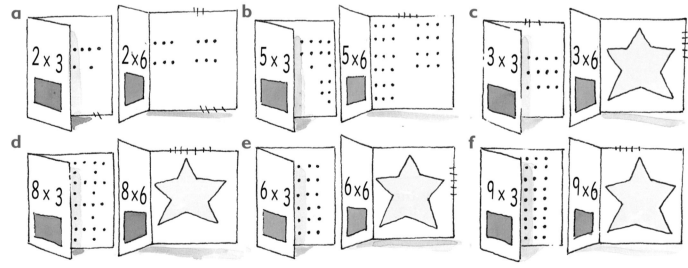

a $36 \div 6 = \boxed{}$ b $18 \div 6 = \boxed{}$ c $24 \div 6 = \boxed{}$ d $60 \div 6 = \boxed{}$ e $12 \div 6 = \boxed{}$

f $\boxed{} \div 6 = 5$ g $\boxed{} \div 6 = 1$ h $\boxed{} \div 6 = 8$ i $\boxed{} \div 6 = 7$ j $\boxed{} \div 6 = 9$

The 6 times table

● **Know the 6 times table**

$1 \times 6 = 6$

Use the key facts for the 6 times table to work out the answers to the calculations.

a
$2 \times 6 = \boxed{}$
$10 \times 6 = \boxed{}$
$1 \times 6 = \boxed{}$
$5 \times 6 = \boxed{}$

b
$9 \times 6 = \boxed{}$
$6 \times 6 = \boxed{}$
$3 \times 6 = \boxed{}$
$7 \times 6 = \boxed{}$

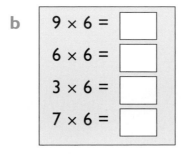

c
$0 \times 6 = \boxed{}$
$4 \times 6 = \boxed{}$
$11 \times 6 = \boxed{}$
$8 \times 6 = \boxed{}$

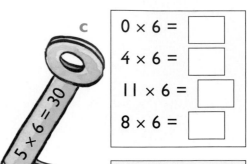

$5 \times 6 = 30$

$2 \times 6 = 12$

d
$\boxed{} \times 6 = 24$
$\boxed{} \times 6 = 42$
$\boxed{} \times 6 = 60$

e
$6 \times \boxed{} = 6$
$6 \times \boxed{} = 54$
$6 \times \boxed{} = 30$

f
$3 \times \boxed{} = 18$
$\boxed{} \times 6 = 36$
$\boxed{} \times 6 = 12$

$10 \times 6 = 60$

Use the strategy $\times 6 = \times 4 \text{ add} \times 2$ to find the answers.

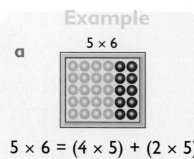

Example

a 5×6

$5 \times 6 = (4 \times 5) + (2 \times 5)$
$\qquad = 20 + 10$
$\qquad = 30$

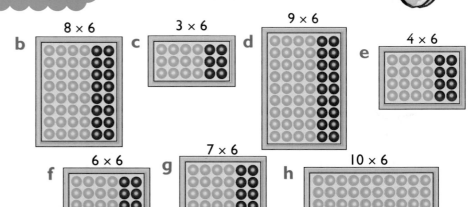

b 8×6
c 3×6
d 9×6
e 4×6
f 6×6
g 7×6
h 10×6

I know that 6 times 7 is 42. From this fact I also know these facts…

$6 \times 7 = 42$
$42 \div 6 = 7$
$70 \times 6 = 420$
$420 \div 60 = 7$

● Choose a different 6 times table fact.

● Write as many related facts as you can.

● How many related facts do you know?

● Choose another 6 times table fact and see if you can write even more related facts.

Easy eights

● **Work out the 8 times table facts by doubling the 4 times table**

Find all the multiples of 4 in the sweet jar.
Then write the times table fact for each multiple.

Complete each times table fact for 4.
Look inside each card to find a times table fact for 8.
Double your first answer to complete the times table fact for 8.

a 2×4 2×8

b 5×4 5×8

c 3×4 3×8

d 8×4 8×8

e 6×4 6×8

f 9×4 9×8

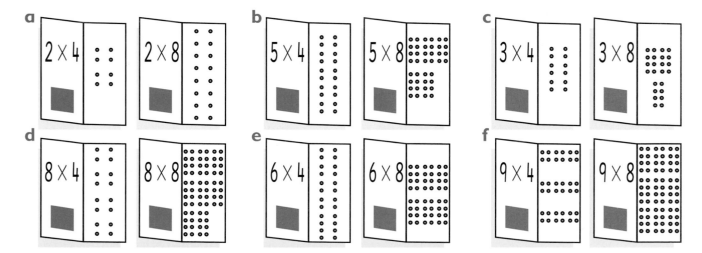

Copy and complete the division calculations.

a $64 \div 8 = \boxed{}$ **b** $24 \div 8 = \boxed{}$ **c** $56 \div 8 = \boxed{}$ **d** $80 \div 8 = \boxed{}$ **e** $32 \div 8 = \boxed{}$

f $\boxed{} \div 8 = 9$ **g** $\boxed{} \div 8 = 1$ **h** $\boxed{} \div 8 = 2$ **i** $\boxed{} \div 8 = 8$ **j** $\boxed{} \div 8 = 5$

The 8 times table

$2 \times 8 = 16$

● **Know the 8 times table**

 Use the key facts for the 8 times table to work out the answers to the calculations.

a
$5 \times 8 = $ ☐
$1 \times 8 = $ ☐
$2 \times 8 = $ ☐
$10 \times 8 = $ ☐

b
$6 \times 8 = $ ☐
$3 \times 8 = $ ☐
$7 \times 8 = $ ☐
$9 \times 8 = $ ☐

c
$4 \times 8 = $ ☐
$0 \times 8 = $ ☐
$8 \times 8 = $ ☐
$11 \times 8 = $ ☐

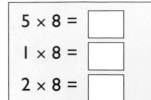
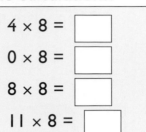

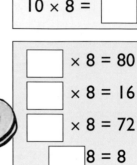

d
☐ $\times 8 = 80$
☐ $\times 8 = 16$
☐ $\times 8 = 72$
☐ $8 = 8$

e
$8 \times$ ☐ $= 0$
$8 \times$ ☐ $= 80$
$8 \times$ ☐ $= 64$
$8 \times$ ☐ $= 88$

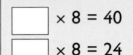

f
☐ $\times 8 = 40$
☐ $\times 8 = 24$
$4 \times$ ☐ $= 32$
$9 \times$ ☐ $= 72$

 Complete each times table fact for 4.
Double your answer to complete the multiplication fact for 8.

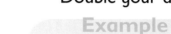

Example

$3 \times 8 = $

$3 \times 4 = 12$
Double $12 = 24$
$3 \times 8 = 24$

a $8 \times 8 = $

b $6 \times 8 = $

c $9 \times 8 = $

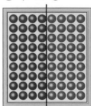

d $7 \times 8 = $

e $4 \times 8 = $

f $5 \times 8 = $

g $10 \times 8 = $

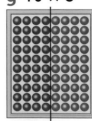

I know that 8 multiplied by 4 equals 32. From this fact I also know these facts...

$8 \times 4 = 32$
$32 \div 4 = 8$
$8 \times 40 = 320$
$3200 \div 80 = 40$
$\frac{1}{4} \times 32 = 8$

Choose a different 8 times table fact. Write as many related facts as you can. How many related facts do you know? Choose another 8 times table fact and see if you can write even more related facts.

A question of sport

● **Solve one-step and two-step word problems**

Decide which operation you would use to answer each problem.

a Goggles cost **?**. Mike buys **?** pairs. How much does he spend?

c Sarah buys a swimming cap and a kickboard. How much does she spend?

e Mrs Ryan has £**?**. She pays **?** to go swimming. How much change does she get?

b It costs **?** for **?** children to enter the pool. How much did it cost each child?

d A box of swimming caps costs **?**. Each cap costs **?**. How many caps in a box?

f Kickboards cost **?** each. How much does it cost for **?**?

Decide which operation you will use to answer each problem. Then calculate the answer.

a There are 6 people in the Kelly family. They all hire a pair of boots for the day. How much does it cost altogether?

b There are 8 children in the ski school group. Each child hires boots and skis for half a day. What is the cost for each child? What is the cost for the whole group?

c Mum, Dad and 2 children go skiing for 1 day. They each hire boots, skis and poles. What is the total cost? What is the total cost for 2 days?

d Jim has £80. How many full days can he ski for? How many half days can he ski for?

e Jo hires a snowboard for 3 days. What is the total cost?

f The total cost for 2 people to hire goods from the shop for 1 day was £36. What did they hire?

Write 5 word problems for a friend to solve using sport as the theme.
Write one word problem involving each of the following:

● addition
● multiplication
● division
● subtraction
● more than one step

Try out triangles

● **Recognise equilateral and isosceles triangles from other triangles**

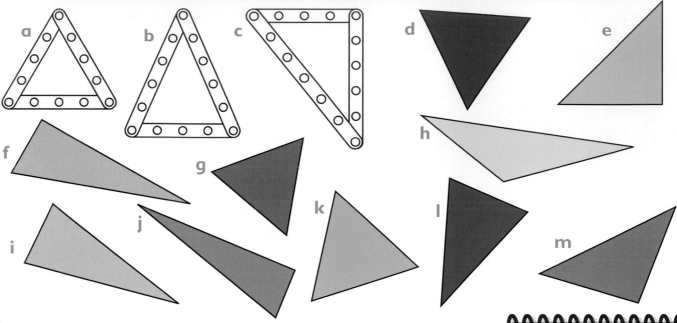

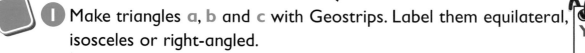

1 Make triangles **a**, **b** and **c** with Geostrips. Label them equilateral, isosceles or right-angled.

You need:
● Geostrips and fasteners

2 Find three more triangles, one of each type. Write down its letter and name.

1 **a** Copy the table and sort the triangles in three ways.

You need:
● paper square
● scissors

Equilateral	Isosceles	Other
a,		

b In the last column, circle the letters which represent right-angled triangles.

2 **a** Take a paper square and fold it diagonally, and then diagonally again.
b Cut out the 4 triangles.
c Use all 4 triangles to make a large isosceles triangle.

You need:
● 6 identical card or plastic interlocking equilateral triangles; 1 cm triangular dot paper
● triangular dot paper

How many different ways can you fit together six equilateral triangles? Draw each shape on triangular dot paper.

Proper polygons

● **Sort 2-D shapes**

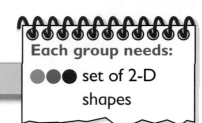

Each group needs:

●●● set of 2-D shapes

1 Work in groups. Use the diagrams to sort your group's set of 2-D shapes.

a
Regular	Irregular

b
Has line symmetry	Has no line symmetry

c
Has a right angle	Has no right angles

1 Use the diagrams to sort your group's set of 2-D shapes.

a
	Triangles	Quadrilaterals
regular		
irregular		

b
	Regular	Irregular
has line symmetry		
has no line symmetry		

c Now choose your own criteria and sort the shapes in a different way.

2 Copy and complete the table for the shapes below.

Property	Shape
all sides equal	
2 or more right angles	
more than 1 line of symmetry	

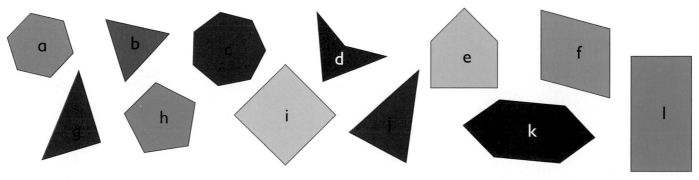

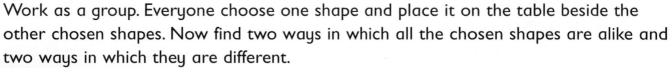

Work as a group. Everyone choose one shape and place it on the table beside the other chosen shapes. Now find two ways in which all the chosen shapes are alike and two ways in which they are different.

Shape investigation

● **Describe and recognise 3-D shapes from drawings**

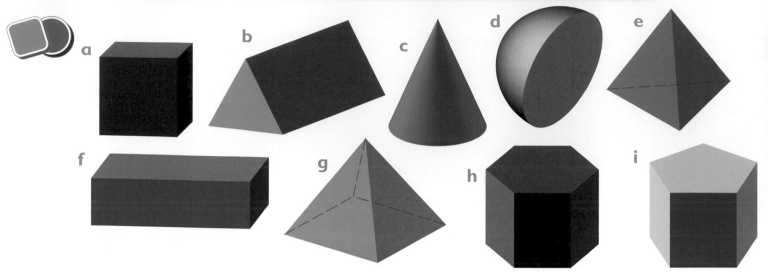

Sherlock Holmes is hunting for shapes. The table shows the properties he is looking for. Copy and complete the table using the shapes above.

Shape	Name of shape	Is a prism	Has triangular faces	Has 8 vertices
a	cube	✓	✗	✓
b				

Copy the following table. Select the prisms from the table you completed in the activity and write down their properties.

The case of the missing shapes

Description:
The number of edges of an end face is 2 less than the total number of faces of a prism.

Shape	Name of shape	Is a prism	Number of faces	Number of edges of an end face
	cube	✓	6	4

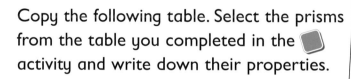

Work with a partner.
● Make a tetrahedron.

● Now make a tetrahedron which is 4 times larger.

Each pair needs:
● interlocking equilateral triangles

Puzzling reflections

● Sketch the reflection of a simple shape
  in a mirror line

You need:
●●● mirror

Use your mirror on this
shape to find the shapes a–e.

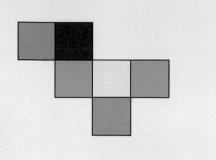

a
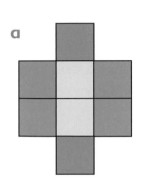

b

c

d

e
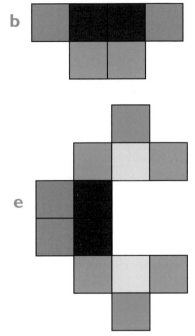

Use your mirror to find these shapes.

a
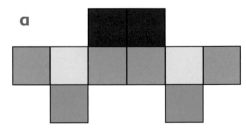

b
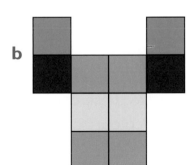

These shapes are trickier. Can you find them?

a   **b**   **c**   **d**

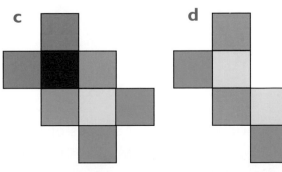

Sliding patterns

Make and describe patterns by translating a shape

a Choose a pattern block. Rule a line. Make a strip pattern.

b Look at these shapes. Decide how each shape is made. Rule a line, find the two tiles you need and place them on the line. Draw round the shape. Slide the shape in the direction of the arrow and re-draw several times. Colour the first 2 shapes in each pattern.

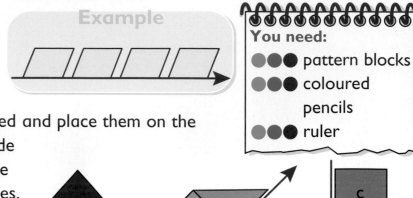

Example

You need:
●●● pattern blocks
●●● coloured pencils
●●● ruler

1 Decide how these shapes were made. Make sliding patterns by translating each shape in the direction shown by the arrow. Colour the first 2 shapes in each pattern.

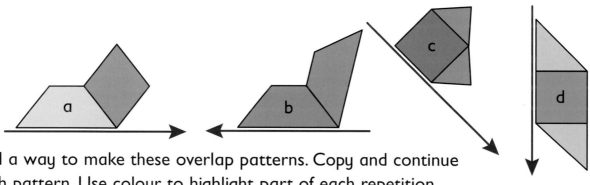

2 Find a way to make these overlap patterns. Copy and continue each pattern. Use colour to highlight part of each repetition.

Choose three 2-D shapes and join them together to make a different shape. Explore different ways of translating your shape.

Measuring straws

● **Measure a length using centimetres and millimetres**

Draw lines of these lengths.

a 10 mm   e $4\frac{1}{2}$ mm

b 90 mm   f $5\frac{1}{2}$ mm

c 35 mm   g 95 mm

d 65 mm   h 5 mm

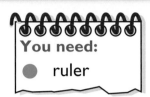

You need:
● ruler

Example

10 mm long

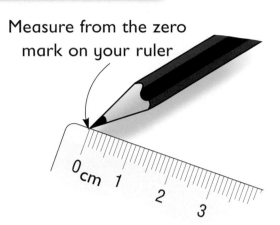

Measure from the zero mark on your ruler

Measure each straw in millimetres, then draw a line of the same length.
Underneath the line, write the length in three different ways.

a

b

c

d

e

f

g

Example

7 cm 4 mm = 70 mm + 4 mm = 74 mm

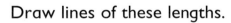

Draw lines of these lengths.

a 3 cm shorter than 74 mm   b 2 cm longer than 47 mm

c 4 cm shorter than 58 mm   d 5 cm longer than 100 mm

Centimetre carpets

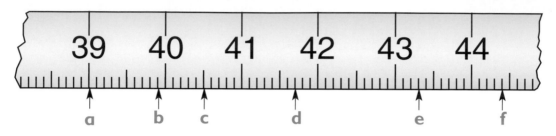

● **Write a length in metres using a decimal point**

Write down the lengths shown on this measuring tape in decimal form.

| 39 | 40 | 41 | 42 | 43 | 44 |

↑a ↑b ↑c ↑d ↑e ↑f

is the same length as

⟵⟶

Example

1 m 60 cm = 1·6 m   425 cm = 4 m 25 cm

Look at each measurement and write its equivalent in metres or centimetres.

a 5 m 40 cm ⟷ **?**   b 3 m 80 cm ⟷ **?**

c 7 m 35 cm ⟷ **?**   d 12 m 57 cm ⟷ **?**

e 420 cm ⟷ **?**   f 936 cm ⟷ **?**

g 2·4 m ⟷ **?**   h 6·7 m ⟷ **?**

i 4·63 m ⟷ **?**   j 5·85 m ⟷ **?**

Jean is fitting carpets in a new hotel.
She has these rolls of identical carpet.

215 cm   305 cm   470 cm   525 cm   123 cm

Write, in metres, the different lengths of carpet she can
make by fitting together any 2 rolls.

Jogging in metres

● Know the equivalent of $\frac{1}{2}$, $\frac{1}{4}$, $\frac{3}{4}$ and $\frac{1}{10}$ of 1 km in m, 1 m in cm

1 Write these lengths as a decimal fraction of a metre.

a 10 cm   b 50 cm   c 30 cm

d 90 cm   e 100 mm   f 500 mm

g 800 mm   h 700 mm

Remember: 10 cm = 0·1 m.

2 Copy and complete this table by writing the equivalent measurements.

mm	cm	m
100 mm	10 cm	0·1 m
200 mm		0·2 m
	30 cm	
		0·6 m

1 Look at this three-way relationship.
Draw a triangle relationship for the measurements below.

a 400 mm   b 50 cm   c 0·7 m

d 600 mm   e 90 cm   f 1·2 m

is the same as

300 mm   30 cm   0·3 m

2 Copy and complete the table by writing the equivalent measurements.

km	m
$\frac{1}{2}$ km	500 m
$\frac{1}{4}$ km	
	100 m
$\frac{3}{4}$ km	
$\frac{7}{10}$ km	
	900 m

3 Put these distances in order starting with the shortest.

960 m
1·0 km
$\frac{3}{4}$ km
906 m
1$\frac{1}{4}$ km
0·9 km
1 km 100 m

Work with a partner.

Using fraction and decimal notation, each person makes a list of 8 distances between 700 m and 1500 m. When you have done this, swap sheets and ask your partner to order the distances, shortest to longest. Then swap sheets again and check each other's answers.

You each need:
● paper

Shopping tallies

● **Collect data and present it in a tally chart**

Mary asked people questions about shopping. She made a tally chart for each question. Copy the tally charts and write the frequencies. Then answer the questions for each chart.

1 a How many people shop at a mini-market?
   b What is the frequency for the supermarket?
   c What is the lowest frequency? What does this mean?
   d How many people did Mary ask altogether?

Which shop do you go to?

Shop	Tally	Frequency
mini-market	ℍℋℋ	
supermarket	ℍℋℋ ℍℋℋ |||	
deli	ℍℋℋ ||	
corner shop	ℍℋℋ ℍℋℋ ℍℋℋ |||	

2 a Which is the most popular place to buy bread from?
   b How many people did Mary ask altogether?
   c How many more people bought bread from the baker than the milkman?

Where do you buy bread from?

Shop	Tally	Frequency
supermarket	ℍℋℋ ℍℋℋ ℍℋℋ		
baker	ℍℋℋ ℍℋℋ ||	
milkman	ℍℋℋ	
other shop	ℍℋℋ ||||	

3 Mary has rubbed out her tally marks.
   a Copy and complete the tally chart.
   b How many more people bought brown bread than wholemeal?
   c Which bread had the highest frequency? What does this mean?

What kind of bread do you buy?

Bread	Tally	Frequency
white		23
brown		13
wholemeal		9
granary		10

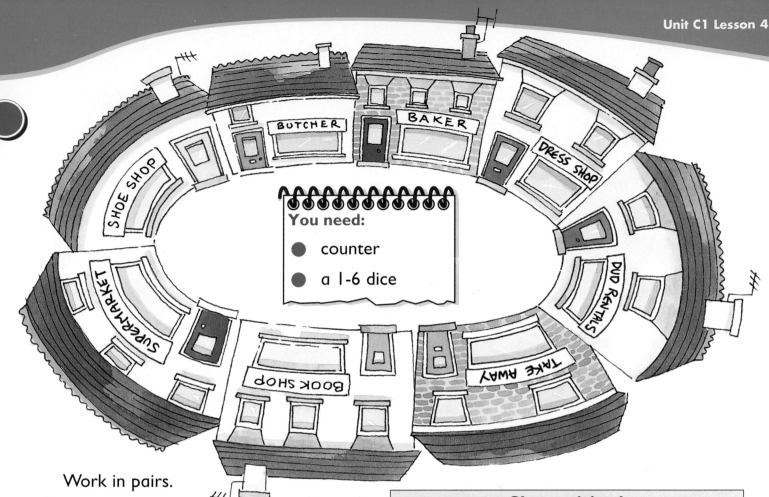

Work in pairs.

1 Play the Shopping game.
- Copy the tally chart.
- Put the counter on a shop.
- Roll the dice and move clockwise.
- Make a tally mark for each shop you land on.
- Stop when one shop has 15 tally marks.

2 Complete your tally chart, then answer the questions.
- **a** Which shop did you visit most?
- **b** What is the lowest frequency? What does this mean?

Shops visited		
Shop	**Tally**	**Frequency**
Shoe shop		
Butcher		
Baker		
Dress shop		
DVD rentals		
Take away		
Book shop		
Supermarket		

3 Write 3 sentences about the information presented in your tally chart.

You need:
- paper

Work with a partner.

Investigate which supermarkets most families regularly shop at.

Make a list of the four most popular supermarkets and draw a tally chart.

Ask everyone in the class which supermarket their family regularly shops at.

Collect the information in the tally chart.

Complete the tally chart and write three sentences about what you have found out.

Musical pictograms

You need:
● squared paper
● ruler

1 Count the instruments then complete the tally chart.

Instrument	Tally	Frequency
violin		
clarinet		
trombone		
piano		

2 Copy and complete the pictogram at the bottom of the page.

3 a How many violins are there?

b Which is the least common instrument?

c Which instrument has a frequency of 14?

d What is the highest frequency? What does your answer mean?

4 Write 2 sentences about the information presented in your pictogram.

Musical instruments

Key

♫ = 2 instruments

Number of instruments

1 Count the tickets sold for each row then complete the frequency table.

Row	Frequency
A	
B	13
C	
D	

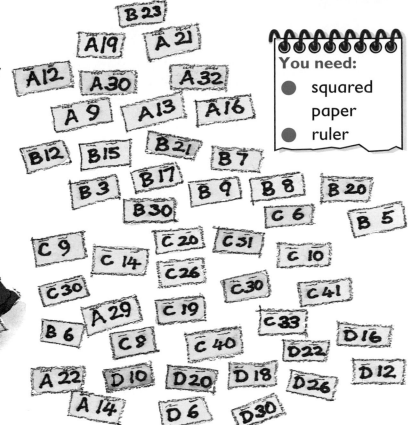

2 Copy and complete the pictogram at the bottom of the page.

3 Draw a simple picture for every 2 tickets, then complete the key.

4 a How many tickets were sold for row A?
  b Which row has most tickets sold?
  c Which row has a frequency of 11?
  d What is the lowest frequency? What does your answer mean?

5 Write 2 sentences about the information presented in your pictogram.

Concert tickets sold

Row

A

B

C

D

Number of tickets

Key

Draw a bar chart for the concert tickets sold.

Questionnaire bar charts

● **Present data in a bar chart**

Questionnaire

Which country
would you like to
go to for a holiday?

Tick one box.

Germany ☐   France ☐

Spain ☐   Italy ☐

You need:
● squared paper
● ruler
● coloured pencil

1 The bar chart shows children's favourite
country to go to for a holiday.

a Copy the bar chart.
b 12 children chose Germany. Draw the bar.
c How many children chose Spain?
d Which is the most popular country?
e Which is the least popular country?
f How many more children chose France
   than Italy?

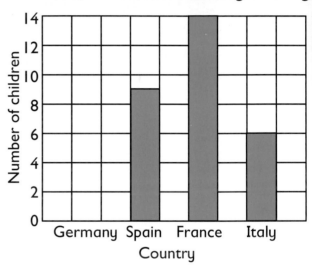

Children's favourite holiday country

2 This bar chart shows adults' favourite
country to go to for a holiday.
a How many adults chose Germany?
b How many more adults chose Spain than
   Germany?
c How many adults completed the
   questionnaire?
d Is the most popular country the same as
   for the children? How do you know?
e Is the least popular country the same as
   for the children? How do you know?

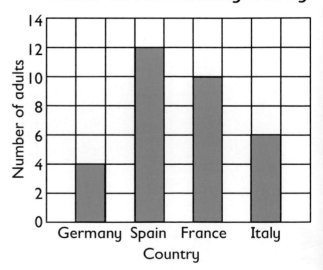

Adults' favourite holiday country

The frequency table shows Class 4A children's favourite after school clubs.

Club	Number of children
Sport	11
Chess	7
Drama	8
ICT	9

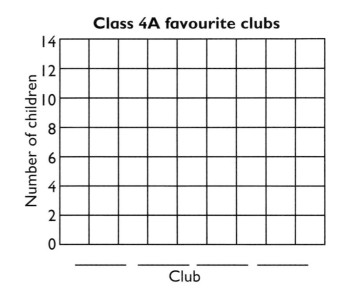

Questionnaire

Which after school club do you like best?

Tick one box only.

Sport ☐   Drama ☐

Chess ☐   ICT ☐

1 a Copy these axes and complete the bar chart.

b Which club is the most popular?

c Which club is the least popular?

d More children chose Sport than Chess. How many more?

e How many chose Chess or Drama?

f How many children answered the questionnaire?

g Which are the two favourite clubs?

Class 4A favourite clubs

This bar chart shows Class 4B children's favourite after school clubs.

2 a Draw a frequency table to show the number of children choosing each club.

b Write down two sentences comparing Class 4A with Class 4B.

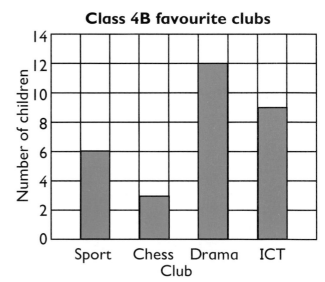

Class 4B favourite clubs

● Make up your own questionnaire with four tick boxes.

● Collect data from the class in a tally chart.

● Draw a bar chart.

Dice bar charts

● **Use tables and bar charts to present data**

Janice rolled a dice lots of times. The bar chart shows her results.

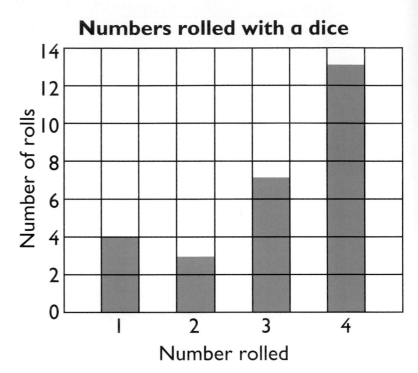

Numbers rolled with a dice

1 a How many times did she roll 1?
 b Which number did she roll the most?
 c Which number was rolled 7 times?
 d Which number is least likely to be rolled?
 e How many more 4s than 3s did she roll?
 f How many times did she roll the dice altogether?

2 Copy and complete Janice's tally chart.

Number rolled	Tally	Number of dice rolls
1		
2		
3		
4		

You need:

⚫⚫ blank dice numbered
1, 2, 2, 2, 3, 4
⚫⚫ squared paper
⚫⚫ ruler

Number rolled	Tally	Frequency
1		
2		
3		
4		

Work in pairs.

1 Copy the tally chart.
One player rolls the dice.
The other makes a tally mark.

2 Continue until one number has been rolled 20 times.

3 Count the tally marks.

Write the frequencies in your tally chart.

4 Copy and complete the bar chart to show your results.

5 **a** How many 2s did you roll?

  b Which number was rolled the most?

  c Which number was rolled the least?

  d How many times were 3 or 4 rolled?

6 Write 2 sentences about the information presented in your bar chart.

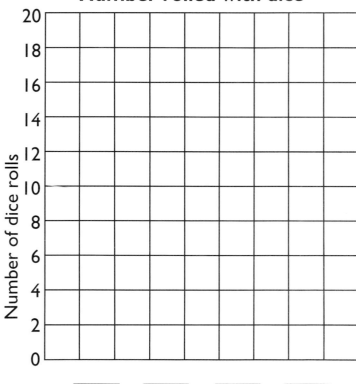

Number rolled with dice

Number rolled

 Look at Janice's bar chart and the results from the  activity.

a Who rolled the most 3s, you or Janice?

b How many times did you roll your dice?

c Who rolled the most times, you or Janice?

d Do you think your dice is the same as or different from Janice's? Why?

Shape Venn diagrams

● **Sort shapes using Venn diagrams**

1 Copy the sorting diagram at the bottom of the page.

2 Draw each shape in the correct place.

3 Count the shapes.
Write the numbers in the boxes.

4 **a** How many squares are there?

b How many squares and triangles are there?

c How many shapes are not squares?

d How many shapes are not squares or triangles?

e How many shapes are there altogether?

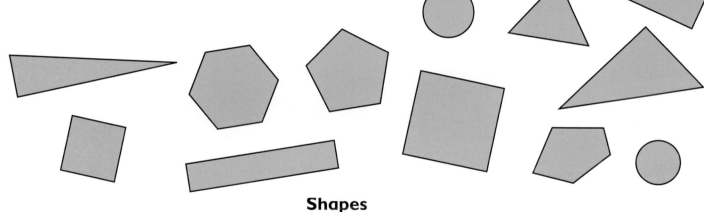

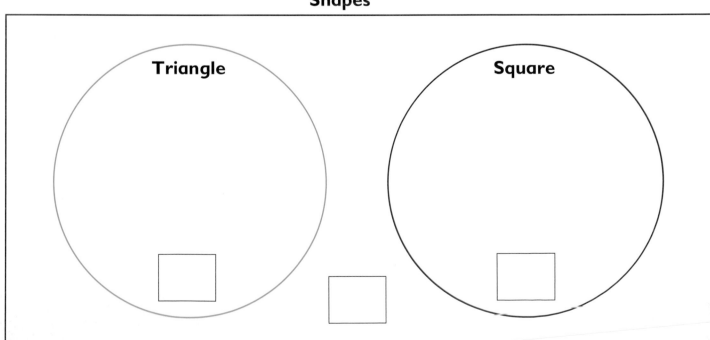

Shapes

Triangle

Square

1 Copy the Venn diagram.

2 Draw each shape in the correct place.

3 Count the shapes.
Write the numbers in the boxes.

4 a How many blue shapes are there?
b How many rectangles are there?
c How many blue rectangles are there?
d How many shapes are not blue?
e How many shapes are not blue rectangles?
f How many rectangles are not blue?
g Describe the shapes outside the blue and rectangle sets.

You need:
- blue, red and yellow coloured pencils

Sorting coloured shapes

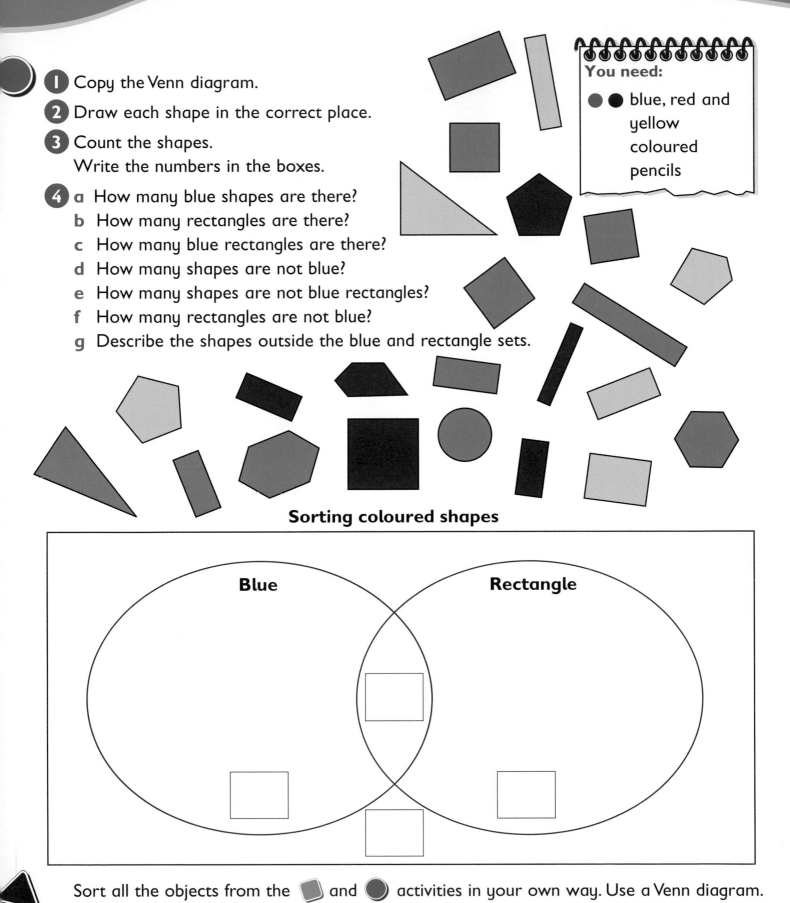

Blue   Rectangle

Sort all the objects from the ▢ and ⬤ activities in your own way. Use a Venn diagram.

Number Venn diagrams

● **Sort numbers using Venn diagrams**

1 Copy the sorting diagram below.
Write the numbers on your diagram.

2 Count the numbers.
Write the totals in the boxes.

3 a How many numbers are less than 20?
   b How many numbers are greater than 200?
   c How many numbers are between 20 and 200?
   d How many numbers are not less than 20?
   e How many numbers are there altogether?

17

98   320

2   29

1000   412

141

135   16   1

752   72   201

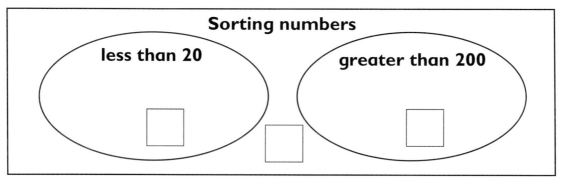

4 Copy the sorting diagram below.
Write the numbers on your diagram.

5 Count the numbers.
Write the totals in the boxes.

6 a How many two-digit numbers are there?
   b How many three-digit numbers are there?
   c How many numbers do not have two digits?
   d How many numbers do not have two or three digits?

231   52   9321

7   500

5   2000   160

99   999   561

4051   10

100

17

9

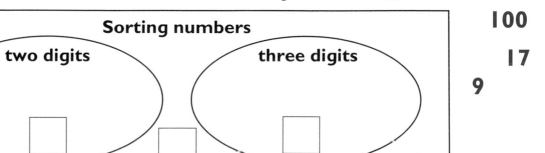

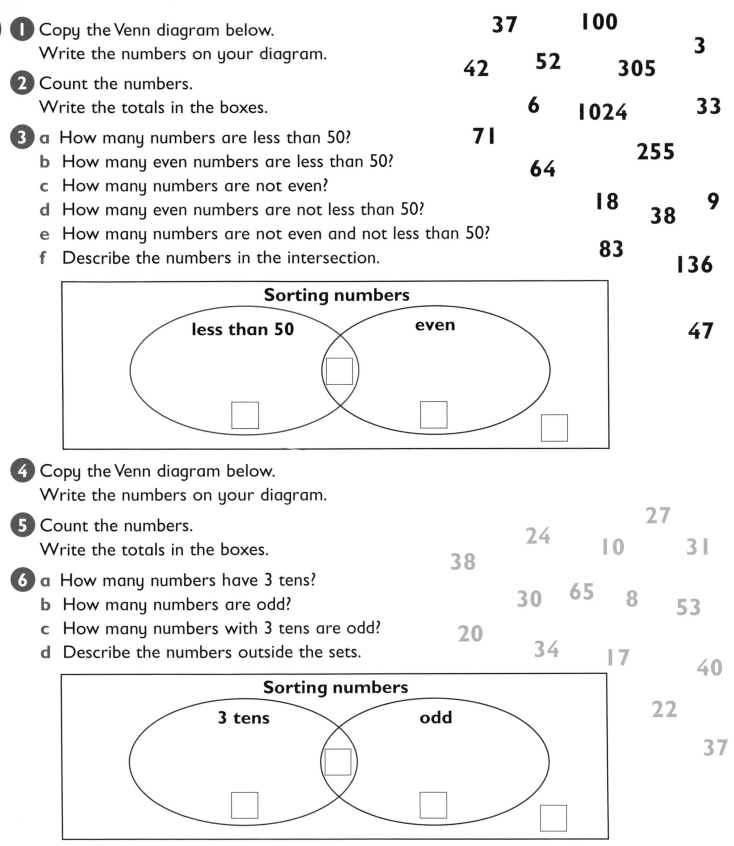

1 Copy the Venn diagram below.
Write the numbers on your diagram.

2 Count the numbers.
Write the totals in the boxes.

3 a How many numbers are less than 50?
b How many even numbers are less than 50?
c How many numbers are not even?
d How many even numbers are not less than 50?
e How many numbers are not even and not less than 50?
f Describe the numbers in the intersection.

37   100   3
42   52   305
6   1024   33
71   255
64
18   38   9
83   136
47

Sorting numbers
less than 50   even

4 Copy the Venn diagram below.
Write the numbers on your diagram.

5 Count the numbers.
Write the totals in the boxes.

6 a How many numbers have 3 tens?
b How many numbers are odd?
c How many numbers with 3 tens are odd?
d Describe the numbers outside the sets.

27   24   10   31
38   30   65   8   53
20   34   17   40
22   37

Sorting numbers
3 tens   odd

 Sort all the numbers from the ⬤ activity in a different way. Use a Venn diagram.

Time for a spin

● **Present data in tables and bar charts**

30 children were timed tying a shoelace.
Here are the times they took, in seconds.

Time (seconds)	Number
4	5
5	9
6	7
7	6
8	3

You need:
● squared paper
● ruler
● coloured pencils

1 Copy the tally chart.

Make a tally mark for each time
and complete the table.

2 Copy and complete the bar chart.

Time (seconds)	Tally	Total
4		
5		
6		
7		
8		

Time to tie a shoelace

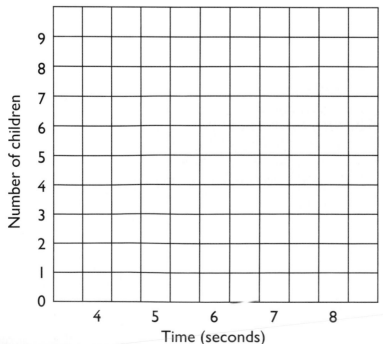

3 Write 2 sentences about
the information presented
in your bar chart.

Work with a partner.

1 Investigate how long a coin spins for.

One person spins and the other person uses the timer.
Spin your coin five times each. Record all spins over 2 seconds.

2 Copy and complete the tally chart.

Time (seconds)	Tally	Total

3 Copy and complete the bar chart.

Spinning a coin

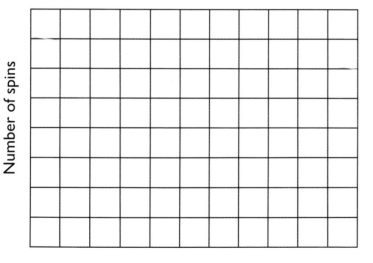

Number of spins

Time (seconds)

4 Which was the most common time for a coin to spin?

5 Compare your results with those of another pair. Write about any similarities or differences.

Work as a group.
Investigate how long people take to write their first names.
Decide how you will collect the information.
Decide how you will record the information.
Decide how you will present the information.
Compare your results with the time taken to write last names.

Leaping along

● **Add mentally pairs of two-digit numbers**

Copy the number lines.
Draw and label all
the jumps.

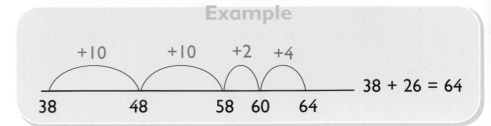

Example

+10   +10   +2   +4

38   48   58 60   64

38 + 26 = 64

a
47

47 + 34 = 81

b
54

54 + 46 = 100

c
65

65 + 57 = 122

d
78

78 + 63 = 141

e
86

86 + 75 = 161

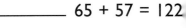

Work out these calculations using an empty number line.

a 67 + 53   =   **b** 88 + 73   =   **c** 29 + 57   =

d 36 + 49   =   **e** 51 + 89   =   **f** 96 + 76   =

g 37 + 49   =   **h** 63 + 78   =   **i** 86 + 28   =

Explain why an empty number line is a good way to record
your mental calculations.

Subtraction highlights

Subtract mentally pairs of two-digit whole numbers

Copy the number lines.
Draw and label all the jumps.

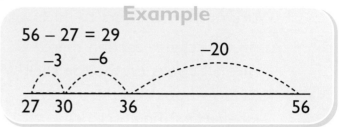

Example

$56 - 27 = 29$

```
      −3      −6              −20
     ⌒       ⌒         ⌒⌒⌒⌒⌒⌒
  ───┴───────┴─────────┴──────────────
   27   30       36                  56
```

a $58 - 34 = 24$ _____ 24

b $82 - 43 = 39$ _____ 39

c $78 - 39 = 39$ _____ 39

d $67 - 24 = 43$ _____ 43

e $56 - 32 = 24$ _____ 24

f $49 - 23 = 26$ _____ 26

Work out these calculations, using an empty number line.

a $76 - 53 =$	b $99 - 67 =$	c $64 - 31 =$
d $87 - 32 =$	e $98 - 61 =$	f $81 - 39 =$
g $93 - 54 =$	h $67 - 24 =$	i $47 - 21 =$
j $66 - 35 =$	k $72 - 34 =$	l $42 - 17 =$

Explain what you would be thinking if you worked out one of these calculations in your head without the empty number line.

Library problems

● **Solve one-step and two-step word problems**

Work out the answers to each word problem.

a In the science section there are 68 books on the top shelf and 74 books on the bottom shelf. How many science books are there altogether?

b There are 124 picture books in the children's library. On Monday, 95 were taken out. How many were left?

c Two classes of children visited the library. The first class took out 37 books and the second class took out 45 books. How many books were taken out altogether?

d On Monday 34 cookery books were taken out, on Tuesday 56 and on Wednesday 18. How many were taken out altogether?

e There are 148 sports books. 59 got ruined in a flood. How many were left undamaged?

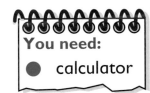

You need:
● calculator

a Two classes of children visited the library on Thursday. Altogether they returned 121 books. The first class returned 65 books. How many did the second class return?

b 127 books were returned on Friday morning, 239 in the afternoon. The total number of returns for the day was 557. How many were returned in the evening?

c The art section of the library contains 402 books. There are 134 on the top shelf, 161 on the middle shelf. How many are on the bottom shelf?

d In the history section there are 184 books on the top shelf, 87 on the bottom shelf. The librarian removes 72 of the books. How many are left?

Check your answers on a calculator!

Explain how you know which operation to use when you are solving word problems.

Measurement round up

● **Use a measuring tape, metre stick or ruler to measure a length accurately**

Round these lengths to the nearest 10 cm.

a 456 cm   b 465 cm   c 546 cm

d 564 cm   e 654 cm   f 645 cm

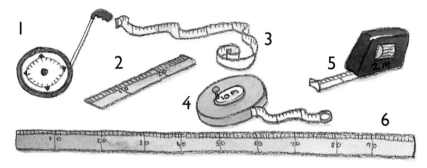

These are some of the tools you can use to measure length. Work with a partner to measure things that have a length between 1 metre and 10 metres.

1 a Copy the table. In the first column, write what you are going to measure. In the next column, write the number of the measuring tool you are going to use.

b Measure to the nearest centimetre. Record the actual length in two ways, then round it to the nearest 10 cm.

2 Now choose two more things to measure and record your answers.

What we measured	Tool	Actual length m/cm	m	Rounded to the nearest 10 cm
1 length of window sill	4	6 m 43 cm	6·43 m	640 cm
2 width of				
3 depth of				
4 height of				
5 distance to…from…				
6				
7				

Add your own ideas here.

Hattie's house is 300 m along the road from her school. There is a lamppost at her front gate, one outside the school and 4 lampposts in between. All the lampposts are the same distance apart. What is the distance, in metres, between each lamppost?

Fun run

● **Solve word problems involving length**

Look at the race course then copy and complete this table, writing the distances in metres and kilometres.

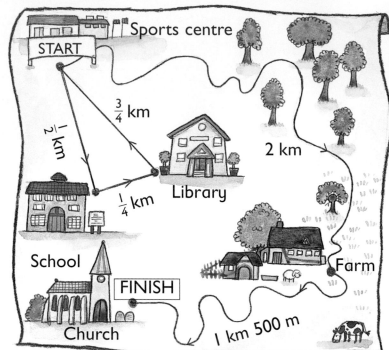

	Distance	
	m	km
Sports centre to school	500 m	$\frac{1}{2}$ km
School to library		
Library to sports centre		
Sports centre to farm		
Farm to church		

Six children have entered a 5 km fun run. Coming up to the finishing line, they are in these positions.

1 Copy the line below and mark the position of each runner on the line.

2 Write the distance in metres between:

   a Clare and Andrew   **b** Bola and Ella

   c David and Bola   **d** Clare and David

Andrew	200 m from the finishing line
Bola	$\frac{1}{10}$ km behind Andrew
Clare	0·2 km ahead of Bola
Deepak	400 m behind Clare
Ella	$\frac{1}{2}$ km behind Andrew
David	300 m ahead of Ella

3 a Which two runners are furthest apart?   **b** What is the distance between them?

4 a How many kilometres has Deepak run?   **b** How far has Deepak still to run?

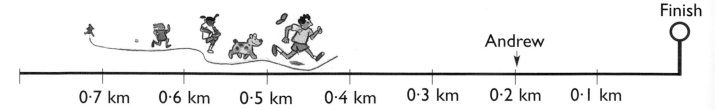

It takes about one minute to run 0·2 km. In how many minutes' time will each of the six children in the 5 km race reach the finishing line?

Up to the minute

● **Read the time from a clock with hands to the nearest minute, and from a 12-hour digital clock**

Write the time on each clock in words.

1 a    b   c    d

2 a    b    c    d

1 Write these times in three ways.

a 2:58	b 4:56	c 6:49
d 8:51	e 12:54	f 9:48

> **Example**
>
> 3: 43
> Three forty three
> Forty three minutes past three
> Seventeen minutes to four

2 Copy and complete these time sequences.

a 5:00,   5:01,   5:02,   _____, _____, _____,

b 3:56,   _____,   3:58,   _____, _____, _____,   4:02

c 12:25,   12:27,   _____, _____, _____,   12:35,   _____

1 The time this clock shows is 9:16.
What time will it show:

   a in 2 hours' time
   b in half an hour
   c in 15 minutes
   d in 8 minutes
   e in 48 minutes?

2 Look at the time on this clock.

Write in digital form the time:
   a 3 hours earlier
   b 15 minutes earlier
   c half an hour later.

Measuring time

● **Solve problems where you have to estimate and measure time**

 ❶ Write which unit you would use to measure how long it takes to do these.

a boil an egg

b cross the road safely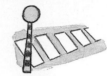

c build a house

d blink

e run 100 metres

f eat an ice cream

❷ Write the best estimate for these times.

a a bus journey into town	15 minutes	30 minutes	1 hour
b a fortnight's holiday	10 days	2 weeks	40 days
c a sneeze	2 seconds	20 seconds	40 seconds
d a flight to America from London	1 hour	3 hours	10 hours

 Your group has 5 minutes at each station.
Make a chart to show what you did at each station.

Station	Activity	Estimated time	Measured time

Station 1

Estimate and measure the time taken:
● to read aloud a verse of a poem.
● for an ice cube to melt.
● for a dripping tap to fill a 100 ml jug.

Station 2

Estimate and measure how many seconds it will take you to:
● say the 4 times table.
● build a tetrahedron with interlocking tiles.
● thread 10 wooden beads.
● touch your toes ten times.

Station 3

● Choose a length of time between 10 and 30 seconds.
Take it in turns to stop a stopwatch at that time without looking at the watch.
● Sit and face your partner. When the timekeeper says 'Go' stare into each other's eyes. Who, in your group, can stare for the longest time without blinking?

Race times

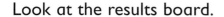

● **Solve problems involving time**

Look at the results board.

To qualify for the finals, each swimmer must finish the race in under one minute.

a Write the name and the number of seconds for each finalist.

b Write the names and times in minutes and seconds of the non-qualifiers.

Swimming results

Name	Seconds
Kevin	6 3
Mandy	5 7
Jacqui	5 3
Dougie	7 1
Imran	4 8
Lynn	6 6

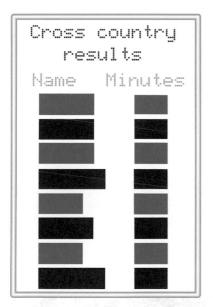

Cross country results

Name	Minutes

1 a Who won the cross-country race?

b Who came second?

c How much faster was Greg than Emma?

2 Copy the results table. Make a third column and write each competitor's time in hours and minutes.

Example

Asif 110 minutes = 1 hour 50 minutes

3 The race began at 10:30. Write the time which the digital finishing clock showed for each competitor.

Example

Asif 12:20

As a group, set up your own time trials, for example, tying / untying shoelaces 10 times or looking up a word in a dictionary. Record your results in a table.

You need:
● stopwatch

Horizontal and vertical lines

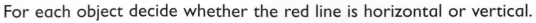

● **Know when a line is horizontal or vertical**

For each object decide whether the red line is horizontal or vertical.

a

b

c

d

e

f

 Copy these shapes on to 1 cm square dot paper.
Draw the:

● horizontal lines, bl

● vertical lines, green

● diagonal lines, red.

You need:

●● 1 cm square dot paper

●● blue, green and red
coloured pencils

●● ruler

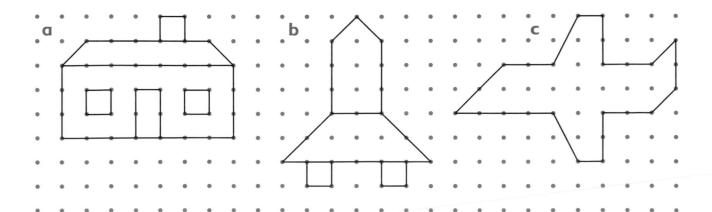

a   b   c

Treasure hunt

● **Describe the position of a square on a grid of squares**

1 The map shows where the pirates are digging for treasure. Dick is digging in square D4. Write the position of the square for the other pirates in the same way.

Abe (B)
Zack (Z)
Greg (G)
Jack (J)
Mick (M)

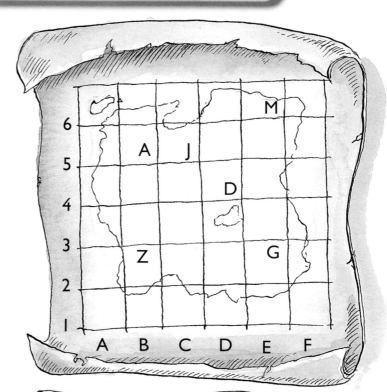

2 Captain Black is digging at a square between Zack and Greg. What might its position be?

Captain Black's map has a secret code. Work out the letter in each position to find out where the treasure is buried. Each line is a new word.

D2 D4 D1
A2 A5 C5 E5 D2
A4 C2 E3 C3
E2 C4 E5
C5 A5 B1 E5

Use the secret code from Captain Black's map.

a Write your first name.

b Write where you think would be a good place to bury the treasure, then ask a friend to find it.

Introducing the 9 times table

● **Know the 9 times table**

Multiply the number shown on each cash register by 10.

a  8

b 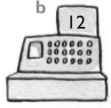 12

c  15

d  9

e 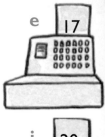 17

f  21

g  14

h  23

i  10

j  20

Use the 10 times table to help you work out the answers to the 9 times table.

6×9
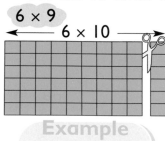
6×10

Example
$6 \times 10 = 60$
$6 \times 9 =$

3×9
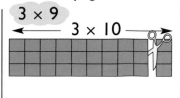
3×10

5×9
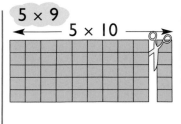
5×10

9×9
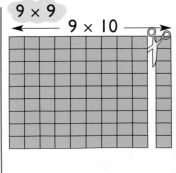
9×10

10×9
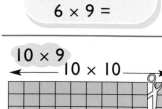
10×10

8×9
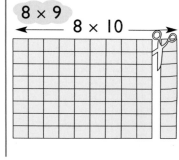
8×10

4×9
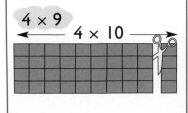
4×10

7×9
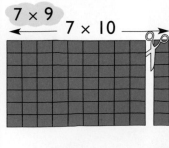
7×10

Liz bought tiles to make a mosaic table. Each tile cost £9.

● Work out how much she paid for each of the colours she used.

● How much did she spend on tiles altogether? Show your working.

TILES 'R' US

Yellow tiles
$8 \times £9 = \boxed{}$

Red tiles
$\boxed{} \times £9 = \boxed{}$

Blue tiles
$\boxed{} \times £9 = \boxed{}$

Green tiles
$\boxed{} \times £9 = \boxed{}$

Total: £

More on the 9 times table

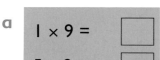 **Know the 9 times table**

Use the key facts for the 9 times table to work out the following calculations.

a
1 × 9 = ☐
5 × 9 = ☐
10 × 9 = ☐
2 × 9 = ☐

b
3 × 9 = ☐
0 × 9 = ☐
8 × 9 = ☐
6 × 9 = ☐

c
9 × 9 = ☐
4 × 9 = ☐
7 × 9 = ☐
11 × 9 = ☐

d
☐ × 9 = 27
☐ × 9 = 54
☐ × 9 = 45
☐ × 9 = 81

e
9 × ☐ = 90
9 × ☐ = 36
9 × ☐ = 9
9 × ☐ = 18

f
9 × ☐ = 0
☐ × 3 = 27
☐ × 9 = 63
9 × ☐ = 72

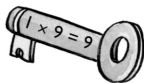

Use the clues to find the number.

a A multiple of 9 between 20 and 30.
b A multiple of 7 and 9.
c The nearest multiple of 9 to 70.
d A multiple of 9 with the tens digit that is 1 more than the units digit.

e The first two-digit multiple of 9.
f A multiple of 9 with 1 as the units digit.
g A multiple of 9, more than 30 but less than 40.
h The tenth multiple of 9.

Calculate the answers to these. Show your working.

a 7 × 9
b 13 × 9
c 16 × 9
d 9 × 9
e 14 × 9

f 15 × 9
g 6 × 9
h 18 × 9
i 27 × 9
j 22 × 9

Example

12 × 9 = (12 × 10) − 12
= 120 − 12
= 108

To multiply by 9 I think: Multiply by 10 and adjust.

Introducing the 7 times table

● Know the 7 times table

Use the key facts for the 7 times table for the following calculations.

a
2 × 7 =
5 × 7 =
1 × 7 =
10 × 7 =

b
0 × 7 =
4 × 7 =
9 × 7 =
7 × 7 =

c
3 × 7 =
6 × 7 =
11 × 7 =
8 × 7 =

d
7 × ☐ = 35
7 × ☐ = 7
7 × ☐ = 56
7 × ☐ = 21

e
☐ × 7 = 28
☐ × 7 = 63
☐ × 7 = 49
☐ × 7 = 77

f
☐ × 7 = 70
7 × ☐ = 14
7 × ☐ = 0
☐ × 7 = 42

Multiply the numbers on the first card. Turn over the card and multiply the numbers again. What do you notice?

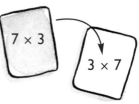 7 × 3 → 3 × 7
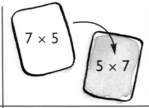 7 × 5 → 5 × 7
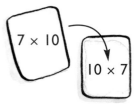 7 × 10 → 10 × 7
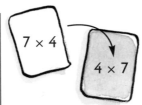 7 × 4 → 4 × 7

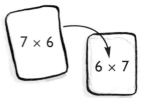 7 × 6 → 6 × 7
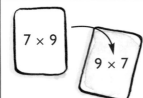 7 × 9 → 9 × 7
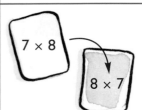 7 × 8 → 8 × 7
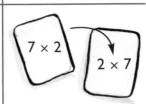 7 × 2 → 2 × 7

I know that 9 times 7 is 63. From this fact I also know these facts…

7 × 9 = 63
63 ÷ 9 = 7
90 × 7 = 630
6300 ÷ 60 = 70

Choose a different 7 times table fact. Write as many related facts as you can. How many related facts do you know? Choose another 7 times table fact and see if you can write even more related facts.

More on the 7 times table

Know the 7 times table

A game for 2 players.
- Shuffle both sets of cards and place them face down in a pile.
- Take turns to turn over the top card and multiply the card number by 7.
- The winner is the player with the larger answer.
- Play 10 rounds. The overall winner is the player who wins more rounds.

You need:
- two sets of 0-10 number cards
- pencil and paper

Round	Gary		Kajal	
	Card	Score	Card	Score
1	4	28	9	63 ✓
2				
3				
4				
5				
6				
7				
8				
9				
10				

1 Use the clues to find the number.

a A multiple of 7 between 30 and 40.
b A multiple of 7 and 6.
c The only one-digit multiple of 7.
d The 7th multiple of 7.
e A multiple of 7, more than 50 but less than 60.

f The nearest multiple of 7 to 20.
g A multiple of 7 with a tens digit that is twice the units digit.
h A multiple of 7 less than 80 with 8 as the units digit.

2 A game for 2 players.
- One person is Player A, the other person is Player B.
- Take turns to roll the dice and multiply the dice number by 7.
- Cover that answer on your row of numbers.
- If an answer is already covered, miss a go.
- The winner is the first player to cover all 10 of their numbers.

You need:
- 10 counters each
- 1-10 dice

Player A

28	63	7	35	14	42	56	21	70	49

Player B

14	21	70	28	49	63	7	42	56	35

- Copy and complete the calendar.
- Investigate the position of dates which are multiples of 7.

- Investigate for other months when the first day of the month falls on different days.

JUNE						
Mon	Tue	Wed	Thu	Fri	Sat	Sun
		1	2	3	4	5
6	7	8	9	10	11	12
13	14					

Musical maths

● **Solve one-step and two-step word problems**

Read the word problems. Choose and use an appropriate method of calculating your answer:

● mental   ● mental with jottings   ● pencil and paper

saxophone £72

£8 recorder

£24

flute

£5

SONG SHEETS

£35

violin

£46

trumpet

MUSIC LESSONS £25 PER HOUR

a Year 4 have enough money to buy 6 recorders. How much money do they have?	**b** Ali has only saved half of the cost of the saxophone. How much has he saved?
c How much will it cost to have 4 hours of music lessons?	**d** John buys 2 flutes. How much does he spend?

a Joey has enough money for 5 hours of music lessons. How much does he have?	**b** Recorders are packed in boxes of 7. How much does it cost to buy the box?
c The school buys 4 trumpets. What is the total cost?	**d** Megan buys a flute and a saxophone. She pays the total cost off over 4 weeks. How much does she pay each week?
e Mr. Travis wants to buy 4 violins and 4 song sheets. He has £100. How much more does he need?	**f** Shamina gets £3 pocket money per week. How many weeks will it take her to save up for the saxophone?

Write 5 word problems for a friend to solve using music as the theme.
Write one word problem involving each of the following:

● addition   ● multiplication   ● division

● subtraction   ● more than one step

Field fractions

● **Find fractions of shapes**

What fraction is one part of each field?

a 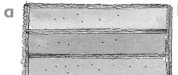 b  c  d

1 Look at these partly planted fields. Match each fraction to its field.

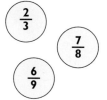 a 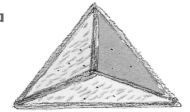 b 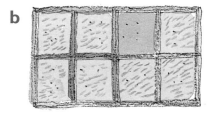 c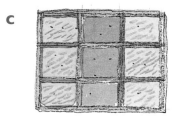

2 Write the fraction of each field that is planted.

3 Now write the fraction that is not planted.

a 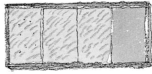 b  c  d

4 Copy each field on to squared paper. Colour the fraction shown.

a 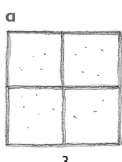 b 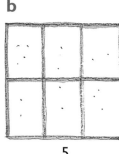 c 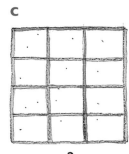 d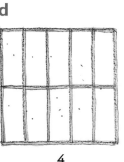

$$\frac{3}{4} \qquad \frac{5}{6} \qquad \frac{2}{3} \qquad \frac{4}{5}$$

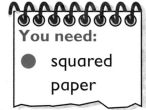

You need:
● squared paper

Explain what the numerator and denominator tell us about the fraction.

Different but the same

● **Find fractions of shapes**

Look at the shapes and write what fraction of each shape is shaded.

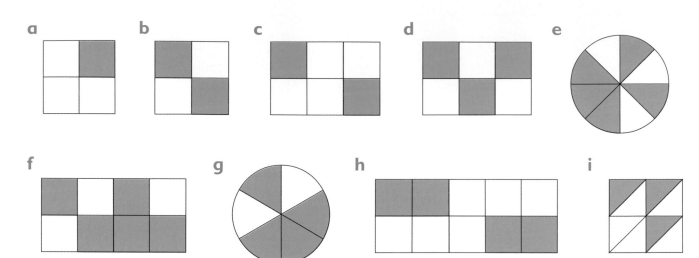

a   b   c   d   e

f   g   h   i

Look at this rectangle. Can you find ten ways to shade $\frac{3}{8}$ of it?
Draw the rectangles in your exercise book.

You need:
● coloured pencil

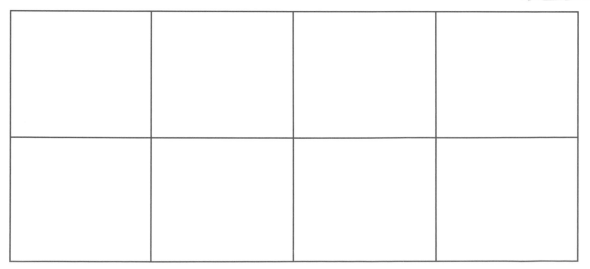

Do you think you have found all the different ways? Explain why or why not.

Freaky fraction machines

● **Find fractions of numbers or quantities**

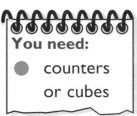
You need:
● counters or cubes

Look at the instructions on the machines to calculate the numbers coming out. If you need to, use counters or cubes to help you.

Example

a 10  5

b 12

c 16

d 18

e 24

f 21

1 Write down the fraction of sweets that will go into each bag. Now write the calculation as a division fact.

a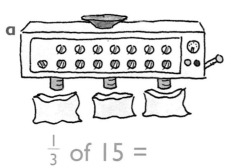

$\frac{1}{3}$ of 15 =

b

c

2 Calculate the numbers coming out of the machines.

a 28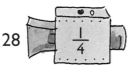

b 24

c 68

 Calculate the amounts coming out of the machine.

a 76p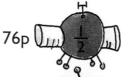

b 24 cm

c 90p

d £1

e 1 m

f 4 cm

Fruit sharing

- **Work out a problem using diagrams**

Emily is going to share out her bag of oranges and she says each person is going to get 4.

1 How many oranges could she have in her bag altogether? Work out two totals. Record your working out as diagrams.

2 For each of your totals, what fraction of the total does each person get?

Use cubes to help you

You need:
- cubes

Edmund is going to share out his box of bananas and he says each person is going to get 5.

1 How many bananas could he have in his box altogether? Work out five totals. Explain how you worked these out, using diagrams.

2 For each of your totals, what fraction of the total does each person get?

Why do the fractions change even though each person gets the same amount of fruit each time?

Half the same

 Use diagrams to identify equivalent fractions

1 Half the bottle tops are red. Write other fractions to show half.

a  $\frac{1}{2} = \frac{2}{4}$

b  $\frac{1}{2} = \frac{}{6}$

c 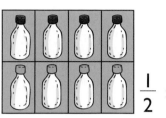 $\frac{1}{2} = \frac{}{8}$

d  $\frac{1}{2} = \frac{}{10}$

e  $\frac{1}{2} = \frac{}{12}$

2 Explain how you worked out the answer.

 1 Write the fraction that shows how many bottles are left in each crate.

a

b

c

d

e

f

g

h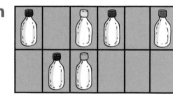

2 Which of the fractions are the same as a half?

3 How did you work out if the fraction was the same as a half or not?

 Look at all your answers for ⬤ question **2** . What do you notice about all the fractions that are equal to a half?

Equal pizzas

Use diagrams to identify equivalent fractions

 1 Look at the pizzas and write how many pieces you would eat if you ate half.

a 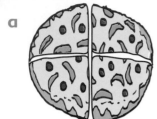 b  c

d 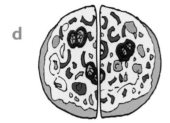 e  f

2 Now write the fraction that is the same as a half for each pizza.

 1 Four friends go out for a pizza. Here are the pizzas that are on sale. Which ones can they buy and share into quarters exactly? Draw the pizzas in your exercise book and put a ✔ or a ✘ next to them.

a  b  c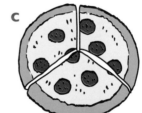

d 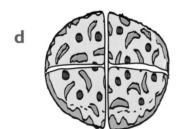 e  f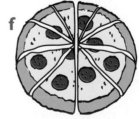

2 Look at the pizzas you put a ✔ next to. Write the fraction of that pizza that each person will eat. Write it as an equivalent fraction: $\frac{1}{4}$ = ☐ .

 1 Look at all your answers for ● question **2**. What do you notice about all the fractions that are equal to a quarter?

2 Explain why sixths cannot be equal to a quarter.

What's left?

● **Understand mixed numbers**

Look at the cakes. Describe the pieces left as a mixed number.

Remember

A mixed number is a number that has whole numbers and fractions, for example $1\frac{3}{4}$.

a

b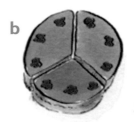

c

d

e

f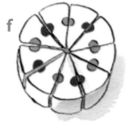

HINT

You might want to use circular or rectangular cakes

Draw a diagram to show these mixed numbers.

a $2\frac{1}{3}$　　　　　b $2\frac{2}{6}$　　　　　c $2\frac{1}{8}$

d $1\frac{3}{6}$　　　　　e $3\frac{1}{2}$　　　　　f $3\frac{4}{5}$

You have 9 cakes.

a Share them equally between two children. How many cakes does each child get?

b What if there were four children?

Mixed numbers

● **Interpret mixed numbers and order them**

1 Look at each set of mixed numbers the children are holding and write them in order, starting with the smallest.

a

$2\frac{1}{2}$ $2\frac{3}{4}$ $2\frac{5}{8}$ $2\frac{1}{4}$ $2\frac{1}{5}$ $2\frac{3}{10}$

b

$5\frac{1}{3}$ $5\frac{3}{4}$ $5\frac{1}{2}$ $5\frac{5}{6}$ $5\frac{1}{10}$ $5\frac{2}{7}$

2 Write each set of mixed numbers out again, but this time write a new mixed number between each pair of numbers. Make sure the numbers are still in order.

1 Look at the mixed numbers the children are holding and write them in order, starting with the smallest.

$4\frac{1}{2}$ $5\frac{1}{3}$ $4\frac{1}{8}$ $3\frac{1}{4}$ $5\frac{1}{10}$ $3\frac{3}{4}$

2 Write the mixed numbers out again, but this time write a new mixed number between each one of the above mixed numbers. Make sure the numbers are still in order.

Explain how to order mixed numbers.

Total fractions

● **Identify pairs of fractions that total 1**

Joe has split his cubes into different groups. Help him complete his fractions.

a $\dfrac{3}{6} + \dfrac{\boxed{}}{6} = 1$

b $\dfrac{\boxed{}}{6} + \dfrac{\boxed{}}{6} = 1$

c $\dfrac{\boxed{}}{\boxed{}} + \dfrac{\boxed{}}{\boxed{}} = 1$

   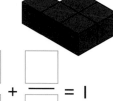

d $\dfrac{\boxed{}}{\boxed{}} + \dfrac{\boxed{}}{\boxed{}} = 1$

e $\dfrac{\boxed{}}{\boxed{}} + \dfrac{\boxed{}}{\boxed{}} = 1$

Take 7, 8 or 9 cubes, all of the same colour.
How many ways can you find to make 1
whole using your cubes?

You need:

● interlocking
cubes

I know $\frac{3}{7}$ and $\frac{4}{7}$
makes 1 whole.

Copy and fill in the missing fractions.

a $\frac{3}{4} + \boxed{} = 1$ d $\boxed{} + \frac{3}{8} = 1$

b $\frac{1}{6} + \boxed{} = 1$ e $\frac{4}{10} + \boxed{} = 1$

c $\frac{2}{5} + \boxed{} = 1$ f $\boxed{} + \frac{2}{7} = 1$

Money and fractions

● **Recognise decimals and fractions that are the same**

 Look at how much money each person has and write the amount as money and as a mixed number.

Example

£2.30 or $2\frac{3}{10}$

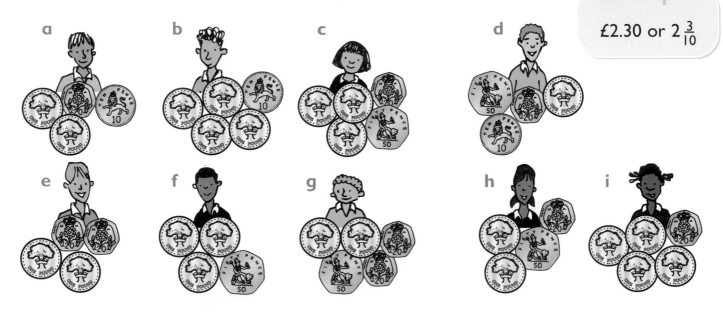

 Look at how many 10p coins each person has and write the amount as pence and as a fraction of a pound.

Example

10p or $\frac{1}{10}$

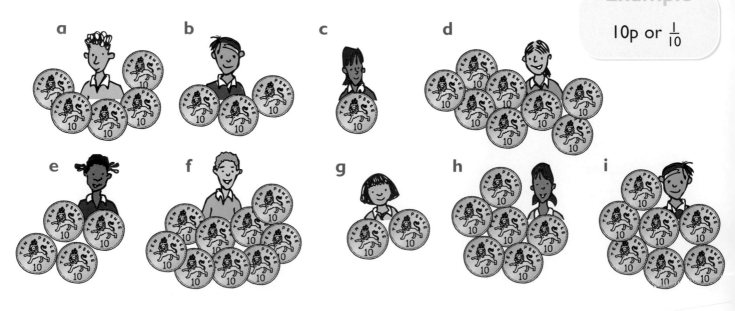

 What is the purpose of the decimal point when we write money?

Maths Facts

Problem solving

The seven steps to problem solving

① Read the problem carefully. **②** What do you have to find?

③ What facts are given? **④** Which of the facts do you need?

⑤ Make a plan. **⑥** Carry out your plan to obtain your answer. **⑦** Check your answer.

Number

Positive and negative numbers

–10 –9 –8 –7 –6 –5 –4 –3 –2 –1 0 1 2 3 4 5 6 7 8 9 10

Place value

1000	2000	3000	4000	5000	6000	7000	8000	9000
100	200	300	400	500	600	700	800	900
10	20	30	40	50	60	70	80	90
1	2	3	4	5	6	7	8	9
0·1	0·2	0·3	0·4	0·5	0·6	0·7	0·8	0·9
0·01	0·02	0·03	0·04	0·05	0·06	0·07	0·08	0·09
0·001	0·002	0·003	0·004	0·005	0·006	0·007	0·008	0·009

Number facts

Multiplication and division facts

	×1	×2	×3	×4	×5	×6	×7	×8	×9	×10
×1	1	2	3	4	5	6	7	8	9	10
×2	2	4	6	8	10	12	14	16	18	20
×3	3	6	9	12	15	18	21	24	27	30
×4	4	8	12	16	20	24	28	32	36	40
×5	5	10	15	20	25	30	35	40	45	50
×6	6	12	18	24	30	36	42	48	54	60
×7	7	14	21	28	35	42	49	56	63	70
×8	8	16	24	32	40	48	56	64	72	80
×9	9	18	27	36	45	54	63	72	81	90
×10	10	20	30	40	50	60	70	80	90	100

Fractions and decimals

$$\frac{1}{100} = 0{\cdot}01 \qquad \frac{25}{100} = \frac{1}{4} = 0{\cdot}25$$

$$\frac{2}{100} = \frac{1}{50} = 0{\cdot}02 \qquad \frac{50}{100} = \frac{1}{2} = 0{\cdot}5$$

$$\frac{5}{100} = \frac{1}{20} = 0{\cdot}05 \qquad \frac{75}{100} = \frac{3}{4} = 0{\cdot}75$$

$$\frac{10}{100} = \frac{1}{10} = 0{\cdot}1 \qquad \frac{100}{100} = 1$$

$$\frac{20}{100} = \frac{1}{5} = 0{\cdot}2$$

Calculations

— Addition —

Whole numbers
Example: 845 + 758

```
   845              845
 + 758            + 758
  1500             1603
    90              ¹ ¹
    13
  1603
    ¹
```
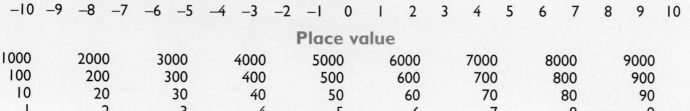

Decimals
Example: £26.48 + £53.75

```
  £26.48          £26.48
+ £53.75        + £53.75
   70.00          £80.23
    9.00           ¹ ¹ ¹
    1.10
    0.13
  £80.23
    ¹
```

Calculations

Subtraction

Whole numbers
Example: 845 − 367

```
  845
− 367
   33  → 400
  445  → 845
  478
```

```
 700   +130    15
 700   +140     5
 800 +  40 + 5
−300 +  60 + 7
 400 +  70 + 8
```

→

```
    7 13 15
    8 4 5
  − 367
    478
```

Decimals (Money)
Example: £39.35 − £14.46

```
  £39.35
− £14.46
  00.54 → 15
  24.35 → 39.35
  £24.89
```

or

```
       8 12 15
    £39.35
  − £14.46
    £24.89
```

Multiplication
Example: 82 × 7

Grid method

```
×      80     2
7     560    14   = 574
```

or

Partitioning

```
   82
 ×  7
  560   (80 × 7)
   14   ( 2 × 7)
  574
```

→

```
   82
 ×  7
  560
   14
  574
```

→

```
   82
 ×  7
  574
   1
```

Division
Example: 87 ÷ 5

```
   87
 − 50   (10 × 5)
   37
 − 35   ( 7 × 5)
    2
Answer  17 R 2
```

or

```
 5) 87
  − 50   (10 × 5)
    37
  − 35   ( 7 × 5)
     2
Answer  17 R 2
```

or

```
87 ÷ 5 = (50 + 37) ÷ 5
       = (50 ÷ 5) + (37 ÷ 5)
       = 10 + 7 R 2
       = 17 R 2
```

Shape and space

2–D shapes

    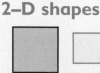

circle | right-angled triangle | equilateral triangle | isosceles triangle | square | rectangle | pentagon | hexagon | heptagon | octagon

3–D shapes

cube | cuboid | cone | cylinder | sphere | triangular prism | triangular-based pyramid (tetrahedron) | square-based pyramid